Funny
Kittens

J. C. Suarès and Jana Martin

Welcome

New York

Published in 1999 by Welcome Enterprises, Inc.

588 Broadway, New York, NY 10012

(212) 343-9430 Fax (212) 343-9434

Creative Director: J. C. Suarès

Editor: Jana Martin

Designer: Hasmig M. Kacherian

Library of Congress Catalogue Card Number: 99-62197

Printed and bound in Singapore

10 9 8 7 6 5 4 3 2 1

frontispiece:
CLAUDIA GORMAN
Three-Day-Old Kittens Doing What They Do Best
Pleasant Valley, New York, 1994

title page, and right:
WALTER CHANDOHA
Guess Who
Long Island, New York, 1965

Toughie
Hunterdon County, New Jersey, 1969

INTRODUCTION

It happened very fast. A frantic call from a friend who said he'd found a kitten near his house in the country, something about a girlfriend deathly allergic to cats, a delivery boy with a cat carrier, and what do you know, we'd just adopted another cat.

I called him "Kid" because I wanted to hear myself calling "Hey Kid, what's up?" or "How ya doin' Kid?"

Kid was young. About five weeks old, and barely able to survive without his mother. He was quiet and didn't need a lot of territory during the day. He played with whatever he found—string, paper clips, ping pong balls, and his favorite, a stray pistachio nut. He did all the cute things you'd expect of a kitten: fell in the bathtub while attacking a soap bubble, fell asleep between two pairs of wool socks and got locked in a drawer. But he was so little he was harmless.

Then on Christmas Eve he got stuck high in the Christmas tree without a single clue as to how to get down. It caused him to let out a series of blood curdling howls which only grew louder as strong hands reached inside the tree to rescue him. And were those claws gripping his rescuer's hands signs of sheer panic? Shouldn't he have realized he was safe, instead of attacking the hands that saved him?

Kid was evolving. Nightly, throughout the winter, he turned menace. At first we thought it would pass. He had a habit of jumping on the dinner table when least expected, materializing from out of nowhere. We couldn't shoo him off—he'd hang onto the tablecloth with all his claws and take everything down with him if he was forced to go. He insisted on drinking from somebody's water glass

(usually a guest's). As if that wasn't enough, he was determined to taste everyone's food. He was particularly fond of tomato sauce, which he devoured as if it had the comforting qualities of the mother's milk he'd been shortchanged on so early in life.

After a particularly messy bout with macaroni and cheese, Kid was relegated to the bedroom. He howled (especially loud when he smelled our spaghetti and meatballs), but we paid no attention.

Big mistake.

Feeling guilty, we let him out. After all, he was so small. But it was immediately clear from the cloud of dust in his wake, not to mention a certain outhouse stench, that Kid had trashed the room. He'd wet the sheets, the blankets, and the pillows, ripped the antique parchment lampshade, and left us soft little gifts in all the shoes.

We tried locking Kid up in other rooms, but he trashed them too. He shredded every document he could find in the study. He overturned the cat box in the bathroom and did his business in the bathtub. For a while we tried the soft approach. We let him back onto the table (we were running out of tablecloths), but he ate everything—chili, chicken, bread, and even apple pie. We thought we'd get him drunk so he'd finally go to sleep, but curiously, he passed on the wine.

Kid ended up on a farm in upstate New York, not far from where he was found. There, from what we heard, he fell in love with a horse and spent a great deal of time curled up on her back, sleeping peacefully. It is unknown whether he tried to eat the horse's oats or trashed her stall in a fit of indignation. Somehow, I doubt it.

—*J.C. Suarès*

WALTER CHANDOHA
Of Course I Know Where I Am
Annandale, New Jersey, 1970

As I was going to St. Ives,

I met a man with seven wives.

Each wife had seven sacks,

each sack had seven cats,

each cat had seven kits:

kits, cats, sacks and wives,

how many were going to St. Ives?

ANONYMOUS

CLAUDIA GORMAN
A Mother's Love
Pleasant Valley, New York, 1994

PHOTOGRAPHER UNKNOWN
Fanged Trio
c. 1940

right:
WALTER CHANDOHA
Follow Me
Long Island, New York, 1967

The Cure

A woman brought in a little gray kitten and said, "Rosie's listless and won't play with me." I put Rosie on the exam table and she just lay there looking pathetic, her ears hanging down. I figured she wasn't going anywhere, and left her in the room to take a phone call. But when I came back, the room was trashed. In one minute little Rosie had knocked over all the jars, scattered my papers, and shredded the happy animal posters on the wall. We found her high atop the cabinets, purring away. I told the woman, "I think she's cured."

C. KALLINI

VETERINARY ASSISTANT

TUCSON

THOMAS WESTER
Felicia's Kitten
Stockholm, Sweden, 1978

The trouble with a

kitten is that

eventually it becomes a cat

OGDEN NASH

LAURA STRAUS
Pippi
City Island, New York, 1999

overleaf:
THOMAS WESTER
Distraction
Vagnhärad, Sweden, 1992

A kitten is so flexible that she is almost double; the hind parts are equivalent to another kitten with which the forepart plays. She does not discover that her tail belongs to her until you tread on it.

HENRY DAVID THOREAU

WALTER CHANDOHA
Washing Up
Long Island, New York, 1960

YLLA
Diable and Goldfish
New York City, c. 1950

WALTER CHANDOHA
Persian in a Glass
Long Island, New York, 1961

PHOTOGRAPHER UNKNOWN
Root Beer Tabby
U.S., c. 1955

overleaf:
WALTER CHANDOHA
At the Sink
Huntington, Long Island, 1962

Pal Joey

Our kitten Joey was raised on funk and motown. If we put on anything else, he attacks the speakers and shreds the screens. Ironically I've been practicing a Mozart piece for a gig I'm taking with the sole purpose of replacing our speakers, which are now a mess. Joey is not cooperating.

HEATHER HARDY

MUSICIAN

HARLEM

preceding pages:
DAVID McENERY
Lost Note
San Fernando Valley, California, 1992

right:
TERRY DeROY GRUBER
Gotcha
Upper West Side, New York City, 1979

DAVID McENERY
Daisy at the Sweater
Los Angeles, California, 1994

overleaf:
TERRY DeROY GRUBER
Chapin Nursery School
Upper East Side, New York City, 1979

THOMAS WESTER
Kitten Climbing Blue Jeans
Utlängan, Blekinge Archipelago, Sweden, 1983

right:

Kitten on Telephone Pole
Skärblaka, Sweden, 1984

YLLA
Kittens in the Air
New York City, 1951

right:
PHOTOGRAPHER UNKNOWN
Hang On
Philadelphia, c. 1942

WALTER CHANDOHA
Let Us In
Huntington, Long Island, 1962

Holiday Advice

Two things that should never be left alone together:

a kitten and a just-ornamented Christmas tree.

DAVE ATKINS

SCREENWRITER

MANHATTAN

WALTER CHANDOHA
Now What
Huntington, Long Island, 1962

Archy's Dynasty

My cat Archy, we used to call him the Unknown Kitty. He liked to walk into a paper bag until it covered his head, and then stumble accidentally on purpose over all the houseguests sleeping on futons on the floor. When they woke up he'd just stand over them purring and kneading with his paws, still wearing the bag.

His other guise was Archy, King of the Jungle. This involved a piece of leopardskin I had, which had a hole in it just big enough for him to slip his head through. He'd wear the leopardskin like a cape and strut through the house. His kitten-mate, Mehitabel, preferred pearls and her own little Chanel bag, complete with chain handle and catnip stuffing. She carried the bag in her teeth. Mehitabel also liked to take baths. As soon as you got into the bathtub, she'd climb in and sit on your stomach, right in the water. When they grew up, they produced a kitten named Eloise, who really is a perfect Eloise. She might as well live at the Plaza, what with the airs she puts on.

AZY SCHECTER

DESIGNER

BROOKLYN

TERRY DeROY GRUBER
Ritz Kitten
Upper West Side, New York City, 1981

44

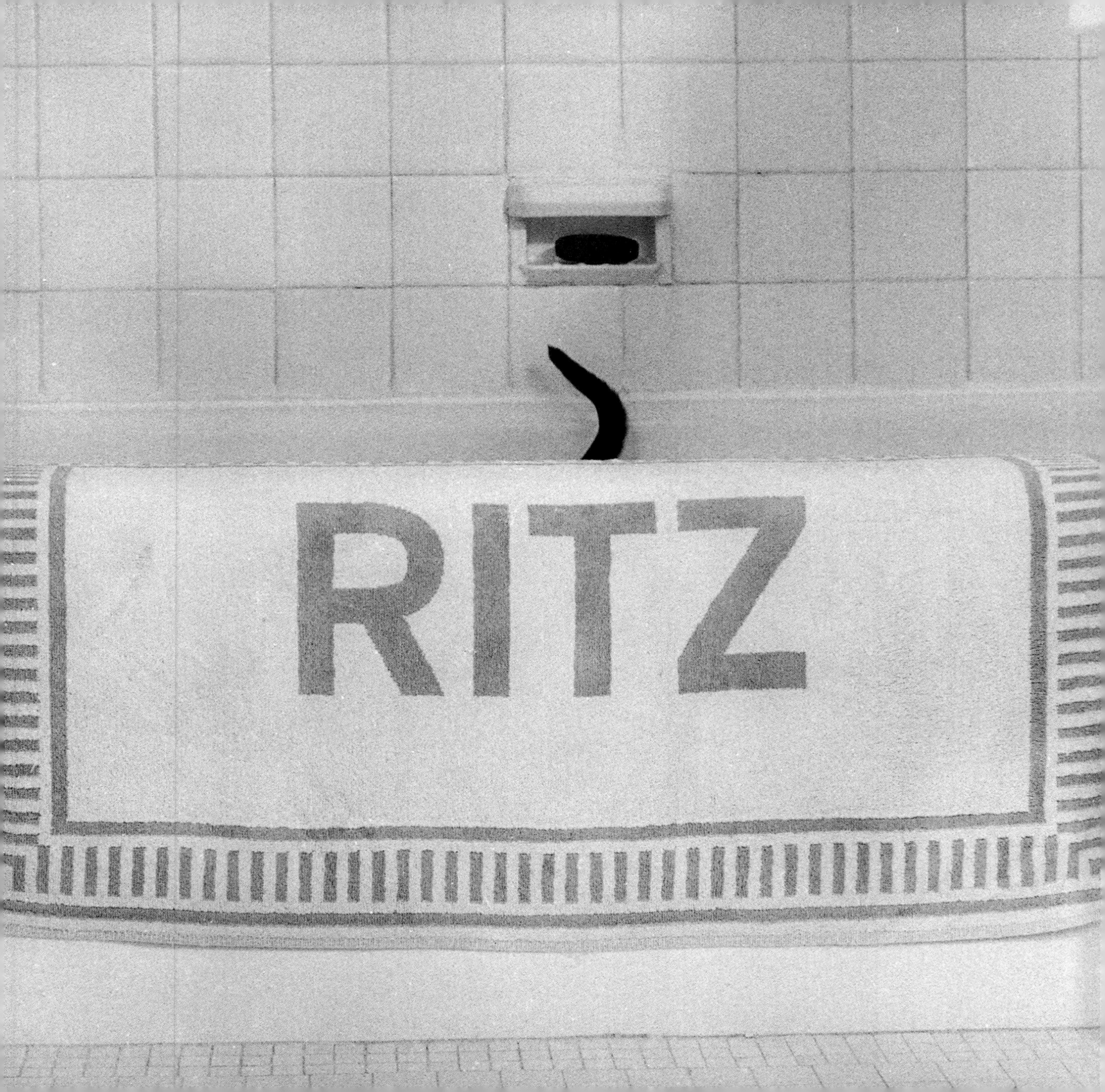
RITZ

PHOTOGRAPHER UNKNOWN
"Farewell," from the "Hail,
Quail, and Farewell" Series
Coral Gables, Florida, c. 1947

I had rather be a kitten, and cry mew

Than one of these same meter ballad mongers

WILLIAM SHAKESPEARE

YLLA
Tico-Tico Encounters a Cat
New York City, c. 1950

Kitty Gimmicks

Kittens are like old comedians. They always use the same shticks.
There's the scaredy-kitten stance, the vampy butt-in-the-air move, the
you're-so-boring-I-could-die glare, the monster-under-the-sheets
attack, and of course the I'm-so-little-how-could-you-possibly-get-mad
look. The gimmicks work, so why change them?

VARDA MILLER

ASPIRING COMIC

CHICAGO

JAYNE HINDS BIDAUT
"Kitten," from the "Animalerie" Series
Paris, 1987

WALTER CHANDOHA
Explorers Club
Long Island, New York, 1965

It is a very inconvenient habit

of kittens (Alice had once made

the remark) that, whatever you

say to them, they always purr.

LEWIS CARROLL

JOAN BARON
Kitten at the Barre, Phyllis Goldman's Ballet Studio
Upper East Side, New York City, 1983

Domesticity

I rescued two kittens living in the barn on my mother's farm and brought them back to New York. My place was a loft, one big room. For exercise they'd have daily indoor steeplechases. Their course was always the same. They'd start on my bed, race across the floor and over my desk, knocking anything they could to the floor, then leap six feet onto the dish rack, with extra points if something fell and made a huge clatter, then into the sink to splash dishwater everywhere. Then they'd leap back to the floor, circle the columns at full tilt and make a mad dash back to the finish line, which was at the top of the silk curtains. The girl kitten, a real toughie, always won.

CAROLANNE PATTERSON

ARTIST

MANHATTAN

PHOTOGRAPHER UNKNOWN
Who's the Fairest One of All?
U.S., c. 1945

WALTER CHANDOHA
You Don't Scare Me
Annandale, New Jersey, 1975

Getting Underfoot

I breed Persians, who are very self-possessed. The kittens are so cute you could scream, but they hate to be fawned over. One of my favorites, Money, now a champion, was a gray furball as a kitten, always getting into things. He crept into my husband Mike's sock drawer one morning. Mike's very groggy when he wakes up. He tried to unroll Money and put him on his feet, which resulted in quite a scene.

MERYL SHAWNESSEY

CAT BREEDER

PENNSYLVANIA

KRITINA LEE KNIEF
Persian Kitten Squooshing Hat
Boston, Massachusetts, 1991

DAVID McENERY
Low Down Cat
Santa Monica, California, 1991

TERRY DeROY GRUBER
Woodworking Shop's Kitten
Greenwich Village, New York City, 1979

right:
Laundromat's Kitten
Chelsea, New York City, 1979

No matter how much cats fight, there

always seem to be plenty of kittens.

preceding pages:
PHOTOGRAPHER UNKNOWN
Dashboard Kitty
Denver, Colorado, 1946

right:
THOMAS WESTER
My Fantastic Chance
Vagnhärad, Sweden, 1992

THOMAS WESTER
A Warm Place
Stockholm, Sweden, 1990

overleaf:
DAVID McENERY
Satisfaction
Brighton, England, 1992

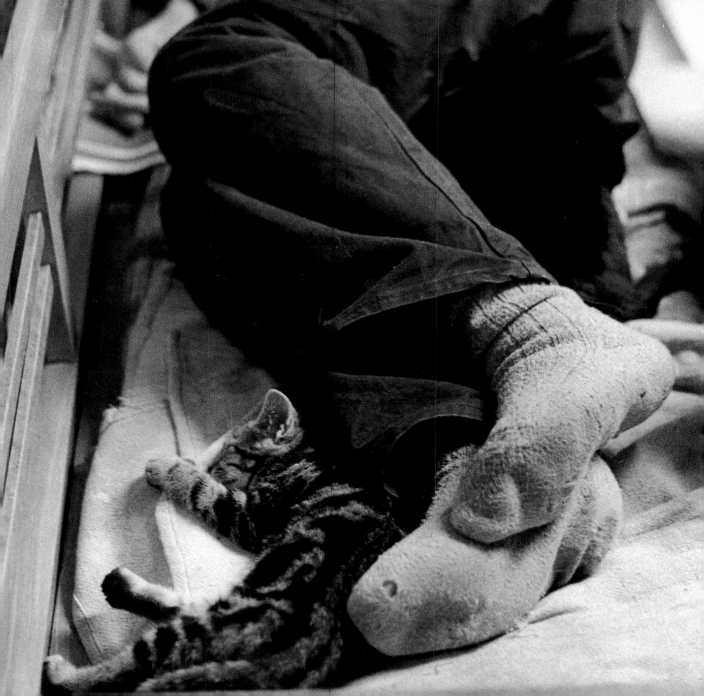

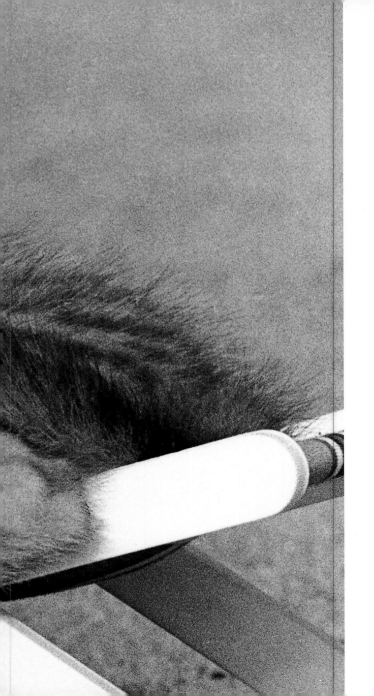

DAVID McENERY
Life of Reilly
Santa Monica, California, 1992

overleaf:
YLLA
Six Siamese Kittens
New York City, c. 1950